Just a Moment

Ian House taught in England, the United States, Moscow, Budapest and Prague. His previous collections were *Cutting the Quick* (2005) and *Nothing's Lost* (2014). He lives in Reading.

Also by Two Rivers Poets

David Attwooll, *The Sound Ladder* (2015)
William Bedford, *The Dancers of Colbek* (2020)
Kate Behrens, *The Beholder* (2012)
Kate Behrens, *Man with Bombe Alaska* (2016)
Kate Behrens, *Penumbra* (2019)
Adrian Blamires & Peter Robinson (eds.), *The Arts of Peace* (2014)
Conor Carville, *English Martyrs* (2019)
David Cooke, *A Murmuration* (2015)
Terry Cree, *Fruit* (2014)
Claire Dyer, *Eleven Rooms* (2013)
Claire Dyer, *Interference Effects* (2016)
John Froy, *Sandpaper & Seahorses* (2018)
A. F. Harrold, *The Point of Inconvenience* (2013)
Maria Teresa Horta, *Point of Honour* translated by Lesley Saunders (2019)
Ian House, *Nothing's Lost* (2014)
Gill Learner, *Chill Factor* (2016)
Sue Leigh, *Chosen Hill* (2018)
Becci Louise, *Octopus Medicine* (2017)
Mairi MacInnes, *Amazing Memories of Childhood, etc.* (2016)
Steven Matthews, *On Magnetism* (2017)
Henri Michaux, *Storms under the Skin* translated by Jane Draycott (2017)
James Peake, *Reaction Time of Glass* (2019)
Tom Phillips, *Recreation Ground* (2012)
John Pilling & Peter Robinson (eds.), *The Rilke of Ruth Speirs:
    New Poems, Duino Elegies, Sonnets to Orpheus & Others* (2015)
Peter Robinson, *Foreigners, Drunks and Babies: Eleven Stories* (2013)
Peter Robinson, *The Constitutionals: A Fiction* (2019)
Peter Robinson & David Inshaw, *Bonjour Mr Inshaw* (2020)
Lesley Saunders, *Cloud Camera* (2012)
Lesley Saunders, *Nominy-Dominy* (2018)
Jack Thacker, *Handling* (2018)
Susan Utting, *Fair's Fair* (2012)
Susan Utting, *Half the Human Race* (2017)
Jean Watkins, *Scrimshaw* (2013)
Jean Watkins, *Precarious Lives* (2018)

Just a Moment

New and Selected Poems

Ian House

First published in the UK in 2020 by Two Rivers Press
7 Denmark Road, Reading RG1 5PA.
www.tworiverspress.com

© Ian House 2020

The right of the poet to be identified as the author of this work has been asserted by him in accordance with the Copyright, Designs and Patents Act of 1988.

All rights reserved. No part of this publication may be reproduced, stored in or introduced into a retrieval system, or transmitted, in any form, or by any means (electronic, mechanical, photocopying, recording or otherwise) without the prior written permission of the publisher.

ISBN 978-1-909747-58-6

1 2 3 4 5 6 7 8 9

Two Rivers Press is represented in the UK by Inpress Ltd and distributed by NBNi.

Cover design and illustration by Sally Castle
Text design by Nadja Guggi and typeset in Janson and Parisine

Printed and bound in Great Britain by Imprint Digital, Exeter

Acknowledgements

Versions of some of these poems have appeared in *The High Window*, *Reading Creative Arts Anthology*, *The Arts of Peace*. 'Lookout' was the Guardian Poem of the Week in August 2014.

My thanks to Susan Utting for getting me started, Adrian Blamires for commenting on the whole collection, Lesley Saunders for our long dialogue on Ovid, the many people who have encouraged me and criticised my poems, everyone at Two Rivers Press.

Contents

New Poems

I. Time Present and Time Past

The Harbingers | 3
Moment | 4
The Spotted Veil | 5
Imagines | 6
Three Meetings | 7
A Couple | 8
   Auntie Rose
   Uncle Fred
Spleen | 10
Laws of Nature | 11
Blank | 12
Taking Flight | 13
Professional | 14
Mina | 15
   Out of Mind
   Et in Arcadia Ego
Afterlife | 16
Pas de Deux | 17
Going | 18
Getting Through | 20

II. Spinning Yarn

Soil | 23
What Did You Take Away? | 24
Another Country | 25
Lookout | 26
My Idle Guitar | 27
The Exile: Mr Stevens at the Barber's | 28
'About must, and about must goe' | 29
Transport | 30
Coming To | 31

Possession | 32
It Must Change | 33
    It Must Be Other
    It Must Be One / It Must Be Many
    It Must Cost
    Something Must Happen
    It Must Go Deep
    It Must Burn
    It Must End
On Margate Sands | 38
Black Square | 39
Arachne | 41

III. Metamorphoses

The Reader | 45
Mutes | 46
Javelins | 47
Europa and the Bull | 48
Peleus's Story | 50
One or the Other or Neither or Both | 52
Pyreneus and the Muses | 53

IV. Now You See It

'Confusion now hath made his masterpiece' | 57
Familiars | 59
Butterfly Brain | 60
Beau Monde | 61
Let His Bones Live | 62
Now You See It | 64

from *Cutting the Quick* (2005)

How I Dealt with Uncle George's Glass Eye | 69
The Glass | 70
Out of Sight | 71
L'histoire centrale | 72
Taking Leave | 73
A Cubist Notebook on Cézanne | 74

from *Nothing's Lost* (2014)

Peregrine | 79
Silver Bream | 80
Light and Shade | 82
Masterstroke | 83
A Georgian Wineglass | 84
One for the Birds | 85
Looking at Morandi | 86
Here and Now | 87
Crushed Velvet | 89
Nightfall | 90
Gogol on the Loose | 91
Electroplate | 92

Notes | 93

New Poems

I. Time Present and Time Past

The Harbingers

Merely a shiver of leaves
which thickened to shadows

to outlines which floated
through twilight and greenwood

and burst into the clearing
in a blaze of doublets and speeches.

Orlando pinned love's name
to a tree in Arden, dwindled,

vanished
into Thames-side bushes.

*

Aged ten, I'd a hint of a sense,
a glimpse of what hovers,
of what's beyond presence

and may be disclosed
in the unforeseen moment
by a tree or a smile or a chair,

a glass of water, say,
simply that, a volume
limpid and still.

Moment

The jaws of a photograph
snap fast, snap faster
than an eye-blink –

which catches always
a breath, tremor, movement,
an action's trajectory –

and the young woman
in a white blouse
with what might be a smile –

for us, lacking past or attachments,
tracks that would plummet her
into a future –

stands for ever
at the door of a shop
looking out

through a panel of glass,
hand poised on the lever
to shut or to open,

a fulcrum, a matter of moment –
the living woman suspended
as in art, as in amber.

The Spotted Veil

Had the young woman passed me
in the street or perhaps on the stairs
and I'd noticed her dress's rich blue,
the set of her head, the business-like hat,

had she paused for a moment
and I'd puzzled at the wrinkled throat,
the mannish grip on her stick,
the veil, the nude forearm,

I'd have thought how to others
we're displayed and mysterious
but still not have grasped,
what this painting reveals,

how what's present, the given,
is less a moment suspended
than a site of transition
from whatever one's come from
to wherever one's going.

Imagines

imago (pl. imagines): an elaborated representation
of an influential person in an individual's life,
persisting in the unconscious

In 1956 God shaved off his beard
and vanished into thin air;

I renounced semicolons, sesquipedalian adjectives and Dickens
and told it how it was in the manner of Hemingway;

I got a bloody nose in the playground
and decided that fighting was morally wrong.

Three years earlier, on Empire Day,
as Cecil Rhodes in khaki shorts,
I had civilised three blackface white boys wearing blankets.

Now the Prime Minister tended his silver hair
and launched a Crusade in which hundreds
of Egyptian civilians were killed by inaccurate gunfire.

While I blazed away hour after self-righteous hour,
Father dug in behind the *Daily Telegraph*;
its masthead looked biblical.

Three Meetings

Now that he's become his father,
knows his father couldn't help believing
that despite television and bathrooms
the world had been sunnier and kinder
when he walked three miles to school,
and back, every day

he finds it more consoling
to think of the man he encountered
the last time he saw him alive,
upright in bed, majestic and smiling,
waving to all in the ward
as though his stroke had released a trapped stranger

than of what he'd hung on to so long:
the last time he saw him,
on a hospital trolley,
a stiff, self-willed, imperious man,
the jut of the eagle nose.

A Couple
after Michael Hartnett

Auntie Rose

Unprepossessing, in the sense
she looked like a rat,
her mouth was a rat trap,
her complexion a vampire's
and not amiable, in the sense
she always spoke ill
of nignogs, scroungers and toffee-noses,
neighbours, friends and relations
and cursed as she was
by the mockery of her floral name,
our Auntie Rose
swept and polished her chill rooms
while her husband went to the betting shop:
'He never does a hand's turn, Ian.'
She gave us Nescafe in thick, chipped cups.

She boiled poisons in a cauldron in her kitchen.
She was a wasp you could not swat away.
She filed her nose each night to a point.
She played football with her husband's head.
She was a cheese grater, a porcupine, unstroked.

Uncle Fred

Improvident, in the sense
he spent on the gee-gees
every penny she earned
and easy-going, in the sense
he never made a cup of tea
or fitted a light-bulb

or left the virago he'd married,
he was nevertheless a charmer
and I admired his hair's piled snow
and his patriarchal greeting
from the chair of state
until, at thirteen, I was bored by
'Don't do anything I wouldn't do'
and the valedictory wink.
He read only a pink 'un
and rarely buttoned his flies.

He was a gentleman-in-everlasting-waiting.
He was a picnic's left-overs on the grass.
He was a fondant with a tooth-cracking centre.
He was as unsatisfactory as a cloud.
He was blown up for birthdays.
He was a cat sunning himself in life's porch.

Spleen

Pluviosus, God of Rain, pissed off
with the whole city, empties his pot
over the pale inmates of cemeteries.
Cataracts of Death splash on foggy suburbs.

My cat tries to bed down on the tiled floor
and can't stop twitching his mangy body.
An old poet's spirit wanders the roofs:
a shivering ghost, caterwauling.

The great bell sobs and sobs; a smoky
log spits in time to a wheezing clock.
A dropsical old hag hands down

a pack of greasy cards; the Queen of Spades
and that charmer, the Jack of Hearts,
make snide remarks about their old affairs.

Baudelaire, 'Le Spleen' ('Pluviôse, irrité ...')

Laws of Nature

That afternoon the breeze flopped along,
expired on their faces like a damp flannel.
The sky gathered its weight, forced them indoors
to a room that had shrunk, a room that glowered
as clouds blackened, indelible, fire-fringed.
She flounced, he sat with a book, they listened:
the clock counted their injuries. Crystals collided,
charges built. Words passed, had to,
the return bolt brighter, deadlier than the leader.

Blank

Her going was a white picket fence.
Each sharp stake,
as the train gathered speed,
was a dagger.

Her going left all the possibilities
of white-walled rooms
at which his eye winced, was foiled.

Autumn's russets blanched.
Everything white was surgical,
the colour of ghosts.

White sheets stared back at him.
Whatever breeds breeds in the dark.

Taking Flight

An empty sleeve will offer
to imagination
an arm more vivid than the other,
more eloquent. What's present
is too much perhaps 'to take in'.
Imagination failing, absence
is more intense. We bring back
the distant and the dead
so convincingly
that loss, each time, is fresh.

All this they sense,
these experts in partings
though they hardly know
whether they wish they could feel
as they once did at these times
or are more skilled now
in guarding against hurt
and so they dally
for the appropriate moments
in the warmth of a clasp,
then turn away,
fingers trailing each other's,
to their own affairs
with a displayed vigour of step.

Professional

In the breathless and absolute dark,
her face close to mine as a lover's
(is the after-life like this,
an unsensed awareness of bodies?),
she searches with a gimlet light
to the back of each eye, murmurs 'lovely'
and 'lovely' again she murmurs,
her voice velvety as the dark,

and though she has seen right through me,
through the window, to the macula,
she knows nothing about me
but for an orange bugaboo
and the blaze of crimson and gold
that fences the inch between us.

Mina

Out of Mind

Last time she lay on the floor and gurgled
with open arms. Now Mina's three
and the mistress of space. *Ex nihilo*
one pencilled line creates a brontosaurus-dog.
She snips it carefully out. But as for time,
she's still adrift. 'Last year' was yesterday.
Where's last night's baby-sitter when she wakes?
No end in sight to all her happiness.

Let it not come too soon, the moment
she will tell the time, be told by it,
when her eternities and urgencies
are weighted by springs and pendulums.
The gleaming teeth click round:
Escape, escape, escape.

Et in Arcadia Ego

It's no bigger than a toenail
in her picture book's night sky
or a sliver of lemon
but Mina, at three
less able than a pup
to make her way in the world,
knows what she's colouring in
is the fat-faced moon
and that the brick tower she's building
with swift, earnest, delicate fingers
to reach it   will topple
and the mother is brushed by the thought
that the daughter's bravura insouciance,
this age of miracles, will pass.

Afterlife

Stored in a plastic lunch box
in a job lot of clodhopper boots,
nothing's more delicate
than OBJECT NO: 52/345/1&2
CLASS: Personal Clothing/ Footwear.

Hand-stitched, with wedge heels,
cracked and shiny,
the leather dried-out, nothing
is more down-to-earth than these shoes
and nothing more wonderful

for it's someone's life I have in my hands,
the shape and sweat of the foot
of a six-month child,
holes bursting the sides with her outgrowings.

I could hardly be closer to her
nor further off. Under cotton gloves
my fingers yearn
for the feel of the leather her fingers touched.

A scrap of a thing but solid,
at the heart of a mist of conjectures,
the lives she might have had:
cankered at the root
or blossoming and many-branched.

Found in a farmhouse bedroom
sealed two hundred years ago:
a mother's treasure
or left-over hand-me-downs
or sturdy little kickers to ward off the evil ones.

I cradle a shoe in my hand,
slip it over the wriggling foot,
gently fasten the vanished buckle.

Pas de Deux

Now that she's outlived herself,
sits all day in the one room,
at night is hoisted into bed

now that there's no longer joy
in the body's flawless routines,
its thoughtless performances

now that each step, compelled
from the obstreperous body,
is project, calculation, sense of achievement

Memory circles her world,
recollecting bits and pieces
in a cloud of unknowing,

kite-like escaping the gravity of pain
till tugged back to the centre, to mind's
fibrillation: 'I want to die. I want to die.'

The body wilfully persists,
donkey-stubborn, donkey-stupid,
lies on the bed

like the shape sprawled on the pavement
which might be a man in a jacket
or a jacket sloughed and abandoned.

The body wilfully persists,
doing what it does, hanging on
till it too has had enough,

lets mind die back
into body's thoughtlessness.

Going

I boarded the bus, joined its cargo of bodies, felt the Parkinson's tremor of the seats.

A woman sat next to me, bearing cellophaned roses: *We will never forget you.* GUARANTEED TO LAST TEN DAYS.

No doubt I was wrong but how those four girls walked down the aisle lit their futures: two scuttled to hide on the back seat; a quick-eyed lizard skittered from pole to pole; the last swayed, slow, head back, daring a response to her tight black jeans and gold belt.

Their faces are lost in each other's, the young lovers on the long escalator to light or the Underground's embittered chiaroscuro.

The bus stopped. The Buddha arrived in a pushchair. He observed the passing smiles with sage detachment, then cast his hands before his eyes against the pitiless sun.

In the street, three small boys, their chatter and bodies in the one cocoon, holding an animated conversation with a lamppost. *The present is a foreign country.*

The ambiguity of 'advancing years'. As when the fence slips past the train, it's the world that's changing, not me.

The bus stopped. A woman's face at her window: young, unwary, unshuttered.

I know I'm beached and where I'm headed. Too trite for fiction, in Edinburgh the World's End Close is a wynd that peters out in rubbish bins.

The woman next to me stood. Her hand clutched a pole. It was the hand of my mother as she grew frail. I wanted to kiss it.

The bus stopped. In a suddenly grey light Our Lady of the Snows seemed to slip down a runway towards the bus, her apse bellying through a squall of swallows. Christ, crucified on the tower, belled his pain. The bus doors sighed shut.

        Ghostly brick houses and two girls,
        dressed for the funeral,
        skipping.

Getting Through

Days are what we live for,
then wonder where they've gone,
are at last what we get through

and that's why I shall found a religion
not on the implacable sun or the moon's delusions
nor even on all-seeing, one-eyed Odin,
master of runes, inspirer of poets, who hung
nine days from the branches of Yggdrasil

but on the workaday hammer and iron gloves
of flame-haired, blunder-prone Thor,
who smashed the land into chasms,
would have drunk the sea dry,
and died fighting. We shall need

his strength, his sheer bloody-mindedness
when all that's left
is to measure pills, minutes, yards.

II. Spinning Yarn

Soil

This evening's sky is palest blue and bare
but for the feverish rectangle in the west,
a blotch of blue-black cloud,
the perfect semi-circle of the moon

and once again I'm thirteen,
ink-fingered and sweating
for the world has been carved
by a red-faced teacher, to the bones

of angle and line: the teeming world
of playful light and scabby knees,
the thighs of a girl on a bicycle,
horse dung steaming in the streets,
slipsloppy skates and tart greengages –
the rich soil left as the flood recedes.

What Did You Take Away?

How the floor trembled. How the looms
and the noise of the looms dwarfed the workers.
How women tended the looms with bowed heads.
How, with mechanical fingers,
they hacked hair through combs.
How, once, they must have been pretty.

How the horse-tails set me galloping
over the plains of Mongolia.
How, glossy, bound and dyed,
they bounced on the heads
of huge, high-stepping girls.
How they were cropped and forlorn.

How the mind is numbed, how the mind is entranced,
as the lightning-swift rapier, with the lightest of touches,
a million times over picks a single thread only.
How wonky the heddle-frames look
as patterns emerge and are clinched
by the slam of the reed to the fell of the cloth.

Another Country

Leaving the airport's a rupture
from all that you know. It smacks you
in the face with cacti or icicles,
logos and excitable gestures,
the time of day's peculiar light.
Abroad springs on you, vivid as a fish market,
where, with rounded eyes, you wander
between slithery polyps, tumbles of sprats,
a sawn-off swordfish, a wriggle of eels.
Three weeks on, you climb the staircase
of the last hotel: past the marble lobby
and the first floor's thrifty carpet
to the second floor's grime.

Lookout

For now the city's at peace. The sniper's rifle
is upright between his knees, his hands
are soothed by the barrel and he's posted
in an armchair at a cross-roads
among dangling balconies, torn-off dresses,
jagged whisky bottles, sandbags, dolls
and listens to vanished disco tunes.
Coffee is a memory he tastes and smells.
He knows, he knows, the cafés will re-fill
with statesmen, poets, astronomers, good-time girls;
there will be public worship, evening strolls,
bookshops, bakeries, banana splits
and table scraps that can be left for dogs.

My Idle Guitar

Oh yes, I can describe
how I walked to the end of the pier
to watch the sun rise
over the Bay of Tampa
in streaks of lavender and pink,
one day as a lemony wash,
the next as a ball in flames

and how I walked with a girl
among mangroves and banyans
through clouds of mosquitoes
and saw a raccoon and her family
taking an afternoon stroll
and admired the threat
of the alligator's stillness

and how we squatted on stools
in the *Flying Pig*
and munched brisket sliders
and crunched onion rings
and laughed
at the bartender's megaphoned smut

but all the time I seem to myself
like one standing at the edge of an ocean
who shrinks from the incoming tide
as I think of the 'nomad exquisite',
that buttoned-up New Englander,
who went to Florida
and let the words rise
from the thermal vents
to pierce the integuments,
to reach the quick of things,
to sound the beating of his heart,
the windings of his mind,
his spirit's hallelujahs.

The Exile: Mr Stevens at the Barber's

What can I do you for, sir? The long or the short of it?
High Toned Old Puritan? That's a new one on me.
So, just get rid of the mountainous coiffure?
A short back-and-sides, no. 4 clippers, a snip off the top?
... From Hertford, you said? A day out in London?
Oh, Connecticut? Misery in the sound of the wind!
Don't like the sound of that, sir ... Are you? Well I never!
The wife's brother's a man from the Pru.
Out in all weathers. Dry catarrhs, you're right there.
Oh, you're an office wallah? I could tell that at once, sir.
... So, you collect French paintings? Thousands of dollars!
Collectors' pieces, specialist items are they? I'm broad-minded,
of course, but I shouldn't talk about heavenly labials
if I were you. You never know who might be listening.
Oh, it's poetry. Well, that's all right. Say what you like,
Nobody listens to poetry. The wife likes poetry.
'Oh, to be in England,' that kind of thing.
'Course, we're in England, so I don't see the point.
... Something for the weekend, sir? Banana's popular.
'Musky and tingling,' you think? I've not tasted it myself.
Talking of fruit, I had that Mr Eliot in here last week.
Do you know what he said? You must be telepathic.
I mean, who's frightened of peaches?

'With my whole body I taste these peaches.
Such ferocities tear one self from another.'

'About must, and about must goe'

'Is all good structure in a winding stair?'
On Earth it is. We feel our way
along its cunning passages

for the whole universe is a coil
of energy uncoiling
from spiral galaxies

to water swirling down plugholes
and men have twisted roots
and corkscrew minds.

What, then, can the poet be
but a spinner of yarn
winding to the labyrinth's heart,

a falcon who rises in a widening gyre
through the hurricane's eyewall into the eye.

Transport

In a 'plane you can be architect,
banker, farmer, explorer. I've had
five wives, backpacked in Nepal,
followed song lines and ley lines
through dreamscapes and word skeins.

Your fellow passenger's all ears, wonders
how far you'll go. And you're astonished,
cruising on viewless wings for thousands of miles,
at meeting this other you, your prisoner,
who's burst into daylight, dazed and rhapsodic.

On the seat back an arrow crawls over the ocean
the 'plane's flashing across. The faces at the gate
will bring you back to the life that is yours.

Coming To

It would be fun, wouldn't it, to watch
a left hand unstitch what the right hand is sewing:

one of the thoughts that wandered the bedroom
at dawn, before the corpus callosum had bound me,

before I was founded, assembled, tensed
for the day's traffic, like the cables and piers

directing thousands of tons through clay down to bedrock
for millions to tramp across rivers and gorges.

A bridge has its uses. But my feet remember the joy
of leaping from one chancy stone to the next

and spiders spin their aerial suspensions from themselves.

Possession

Djambawa Marawili, *Source of Fire*

He was the land's and he made it.
His brush was hairs plucked from his head,
the ochres he'd walked for miles to gather,
he'd peeled and stretched eucalyptus bark.

Fire swept across the land,
paths snakeskinned by heat and drought,
tracks and cascades of the movements of people,
not flames, not sunrise flaring rocks to coals,
but the quiver of light, line and colour
in the land's dips and swirls.

And I wondered who it was
at the furnace's heart,
the little fellow,
barely more than loops of string.
It was Baru, ancestral crocodile,
once a man, now belly-up,
flailing flimsy human hands,
dreaming fire into being,
helpless in the vortex of his making.

It Must Change

(Paintings by Paul Nash. See Notes.)

It Must Be Other
The Cherry Orchard, 1917

All we're looking at is columns and rows
of cherry trees. In winter 1917
it's worse than a graveyard, it's a regiment

of men drawn up to die on the barbed wire fence
that pens them in, a regiment of skeletons.
And I can't for a moment forget

the 'loveliest of trees', the blush-pink laciness
of pretty girls, branches edged beguilingly
in early spring with blossom and with snow.

What flies along the fence or hovers in the sky
might just as well be paper darts as birds
or represent the squads of fighter planes.

It Must Be One / It Must Be Many
Voyages of the Moon, 1934–7

In the brilliantly lit
and glass-glittery restaurant
I find myself watching

reflections of lights
in endless recessions,
moons floating in spaces

beyond all reach
in concatenations of universes.

It Must Cost
The Shore, 1923

At night he'd wake, screaming,
his mind undefended against shells,
limbs, trench-line on trench-line.

By day he'd watch the waves, successions
of drill bits undermining the cliff,
of boulders bashing the sea walls.

In the black ink sketches
there are wind-blown stick figures,
ghost forms who might be old comrades.

At last, in 'The Shore', there is mastery,
geometry's perilous triumph
of long white sea walls and sky, sea, land

ruled into pale blues and browns.
There is peace. There is beauty.
There is no-one.

Something Must Happen
Event on the Downs, 1934

What's going on
it's impossible to say
but something is happening

out here on the Downs
where an over-sized tennis ball
is poised near a tree stump:

some transaction between the one and the other,
the smooth, man-made sphere
and the coarse mutilation,

an energy exchange, a tension
of the forces that bind and repel.

It's like meeting a person
whose nerves are all on the surface;

like the radiance of words
as one strikes another.

It Must Go Deep
Equivalents for the Megaliths, 1935

I'd stopped seeing Avebury long before
I saw it for the first time. Nash, freeing himself
from slavish habit and the tyrant eye,

stripped off the old crusts, plumbed their volume and weight,
glimpsed them as a disposition of geometric forms,
as oblongs and cylinders that take space and fill it

and now, looking at what's for all the world
knobbly pillars and ragged rectangles,
one wonders

not 'Who upended them here? how? and why?'
but 'How on earth can they be here?
How on earth can anything be?'

It Must Burn
Solstice of the Sunflower, 1945

blazing yellows and oranges
intenser than all imagining
fierce as a fusion reactor
self-unsparing self-consuming
the sunflower hurtles downhill
freewheeling fertiliser of crops
cutting a swathe
through grass and standing corn
like a top whipped on by the sun
outpouring of nature's juices
ah sunflower outrunning time
headlong career, suspended
at this moment for ever
leaps the frame and continues

It Must End
Eclipse of the Sunflower, 1945

Waking at four, a Humean bundle
of thoughts and sensations
knowing there's nothing
but a blackness, a blankness
and one day the end of it
Later I see it

out there, on the gallery wall
– I'm there but I know I'm a fiction –
a blackness, not now a blankness
but something evil and active
a black sun, a giant seedhead

withered and shrivelled, detached
from its stalk like the soul from the body,
the God of Light and Reason burnt out
self-consumed, self-extinguished.

The fields are turmoils of bilious colour.
A black hole is ravening,
draws vision towards it

towards dark matter's omphalos,
its own kind of beauty.

This is finis.

On Margate Sands

He'd come to the end of the line,
sat each afternoon in the gusty shelter,
his back to the carousels of Dreamland,
his face to the desolate sands of November,
his mind a compulsive spider
and connected nothing with nothing.

We examine a small square photograph of dust
seen close-up, grey, matt and limitless,
fear spreading off at the edges,
a barren landscape, breeding
coils that might be protozoa, tangling
corpse with corpse on the Western Front

and, leaving the gallery, feel firm sand
under our boots, listen to the rhythmical tide,
its watery slosh, its subtle silks
while the gulls weave their ungraspable patterns.

Black Square

Kazimir Malevich, *Black Square* (1913/1915)

Here words must fail: articulation
is what this square resists.
A black square's what it is.
No less. No more. And yet
the less there is to say,
the more the words ping back or are absorbed,
the more the mind must babble,
scrabble on an adamantine wall,
chatter into silence. We 'read'
this blackboard on which nothing's written
as Art's beginning or Art's end,
the obliterations of the First World War,
an icon for a world where God is dead.

This colour and absence of colour
is more than its proliferations
in cocktail dresses and burkas.
It silences the gabble of colours,
denies vision, holds the gaze.
How like and unlike white's blinding void
this lightless womb.

Or is it just a joke?
What any kid could do?
Ah, but your kid didn't.
Your kid couldn't
because it was Kazimir Malevich
who melded the polychrome universe in a dream
and painted it in ecstasy a hundred years ago.
Your iterations are shadows cast by its fire
on the cave wall. As is this iteration
on a London wall. As is,
decayed by Time, too frail to travel,
the canvas in the Tretyakov,

paint cracked and surface crazed
into a wonky honeycomb, mutated DNA.

Black Square, Black Square,
you cannot exist on Earth
but only in Plato's heaven, in the mind
where mind meets its match,
where mind reveals itself
to itself as victim of itself,
futile spider, fly
buzzing for ever in the fly-bottle.

Arachne

Her head was spinning. How much
her girlish fingers seemed to know.
We saw Europa, perched, lips parted,
on a snowy bull; Leda coiled in a swan;
dazzled Danaë. Satyr and squaddy,
barfly, snake, apparent innocent:
she knew the thousand shapes of men.
She was a goddess in her dreams

and woke one day,
fingers withered to spindly legs,
pin-headed, body shrivelled,
in mid-air, spinning, spinning
out of the small grey helpless thing that was herself
incessant and meaningless patterns.

III. Metamorphoses

The Reader

Better, surely, than the selfie's rictus –
fixed, self-performing –
how Narcissus was caught unawares
by the form of another
in shape-shifting water,
his eyes held by ice-white limbs,
by dawn-blushed cheeks,
and realised only later
as arms reached to embrace,
lips to kiss,
how it echoed himself.
He's all of us, readers,
would-be escapists,
who find in Clarissa and Lovelace
our lusts and our tremblings,
the flower's burning centre, its chaste frill.

Mutes

In the library the master regaled his guests
with a gobbet of Ovid: Philomel's rape
and her silencing – *He seized her tongue*
With pincers and hacked it off
With a brutal knife. The root quivered.
The severed end trembled on the black earth
And murmured, murmured without stopping.

Amid the kitchen's chatter and backchat,
the thrust and parry of footmen and maids,
Cook dictated a recipe for Roasted Tongue:
Let it simmer till tender.
Make several incisions
with a sharp knife
and fill with a savoury forcemeat.
Turn on a spit.
Wipe dry and glaze.

In the dining room,
round a crystal epergne heaped with sweetmeats,
the servants listened
to the fencing of ladies and gentlemen.

Javelins

When I remember how often the sweet girl I was,
wineglass clenched, listened admiringly,
feeling deep kinship, to the smooth young men
sparkling about High Art and low life

until taking her dumbness, her attentive eyes,
for a gormless longing, they glided away
to join their tittering moppets

I think of Callisto, lips transformed
to a bear's gaping jaws, hands to talons,
of the love that flooded that charmless body,
pressed at eyes and mouth, came out as a growl
at which her son poised his javelin

and I'm pierced by those men's indifference,
by that young woman's cowardice.

Europa and the Bull

Jupiter didn't let on why,
just told Mercury, 'Don't hang about,
fly to Sidon,
    find the king's cattle,
        drive the herd to the sea-shore.'

He'd spotted the king's daughter, frolicking
with a bevy of girls. Young women
are usually suspicious of masterful types.
So the Father of the Gods put down his sceptre,
passed himself off as a bull, joined the herd
and ambled around in the young grass.
He was a beauty, soft and white
as new-fallen snow. His muscles bulged,
his dewlap was pendulous, his horns twisted
as if by a craftsman, and clear as pearls.
There was nothing to fear in his brow
or his eye. Overcome by such gentleness,
Agenor's daughter went up to the bull.
She held flowers to his lips. The lover
was on edge, pressed kisses on her hands,
could hardly control himself. He frolicked
on the green grass, laid his snowy body
in the yellow sand. Her fear died.
She patted his breast, wove fresh flowers
round his horns, sits on the god's back.

He edges away
        from the dry land
               from the shore,

plants his false hoofs in the surf
        gradually goes further out

further and further
        into the ocean
             he carries his prize

*

That, more and less, is Ovid:
a capriccio of flutes and piccolos,
a shiver of tambourines,
pretty as a picture by Boucher
(rosy girls, friendly bull, dozens of garlands),
leading us on step by step
through a tale of a fair-skinned lover,
a pizzicato of cautious footsteps
and a girl who goes with the flow
as the cello swells legato
till she's out of her depth, transported.
Bestiality, certainly, but nothing too horrible.

Under a passionate orange sunset,
in the blurry forms of late Titian,
Europa's a grown woman, full-fleshed,
sprawled supine, legs parted, on the bull's back,
the bull's waded into the ocean
and we're led in the minute-by-minute of looking,
hearing the screams of violins
and the drums' ambiguous thunder,
to ponder, to ask of ourselves why we see
Europa as ecstatic or terrified,
the bull as remorseless or sad
that he's acting by his nature's compulsion.

*

Trembling, carried away, she looks back
    at the shore gone for ever
rests one hand on his head
               and clings to a horn with the other

Peleus's Story

She rode to shore on a dolphin,
naked and singing. Spray flowered
round her breasts, flowed down her legs.

Imagine her sleeping at the mouth of a cave.
I was helpless at the sight of her hips,
my hand laid itself on her thigh.

I'd always found women slippery,
you never knew where to have them.
Now there was nothing to stop me.

Wings flapped and thumped,
a beak lunged at my eye.
Then a blizzard of feathers

that turned into leaves.
I scrabbled at wind-thrashed branches,
thrust at bark

till a wildcat spat in my face.
Its claws shrieked down my arm,
its teeth hooked in my groin, and I loosed it.

Ye gods, what next?
When she slept, I roped her arms to her side,
chained her legs in a V and fell on her.

I was clutching something fluid as water
that slithered moment to moment
from panther to vulture,

from wolf to crow to hyena,
granite, crocodile, glass spikes.
At last she gave up as she had to,

gave it all up to her master,
gave herself as the woman she was,
gave me the child I wanted.

Now, dear heart, she's dissolved in tears
for Achilles, for Hector laid in the dust,
and the women of Greece and of Troy.

One or the Other or Neither or Both

Fifteen and full of himself,
cocky and diffident,
handsome as heaven,
sweaty from exercise,
one of life's innocents

at the edge of a crystal-clear pool
he slips off his togs, slaps his body
for the joy of it, unaware
of the girl who lolls in the shadows,
combing her hair, painting her fingernails.

She's seen it all before but this one's special
and now she emerges into daylight,
reaching her arms to him,
sinuous, suggesting. He flushes
breathtakingly, turns tail,

seeks safety in water,
glides through the pool like an ivory sculpture
but she's all round him and in him,
her breasts on his chest,
silk-soft legs entwined in his.

Today in the water's opacity one glimpses
a girl who waits in the mind's coverts,
peeps out, emerges, dabbles and dives,
mastering his struggles to keep a hold
on himself, to contain what's born in him

till the struggle's abandoned
in a kind of kenosis,
a full dissolution,
a pleroma,
and a boy knows that she's him.

Pyreneus and the Muses

You're right, we've a wonderful life:
art, history and song –
if only we were safe. But today

no act of wickedness is impossible,
innocence is obsolete.

Pyreneus's hot breath is still on our necks,
he stalks our dreams.

His squaddies were everywhere.
They herded men with cattle prods,
blasted temples, built walls.

We ran home
but he'd seen us coming

and his face crinkled
into that well-known, beneficent smile.

'Lovely girls,' (he knew how to get to us)
'hang on a moment,

'don't worry, please come in
out of the wind and the rain.'
(The rain was spitting. Or was it a rifle?)

He was very persuasive.
So in we went,
just into the entrance hall,

then up to the penthouse
(we must see the view)

until the wind had swung round
and the sky had cleared
and we were keen to be on our way.

Then Pyreneus slammed the doors
and advanced on us, rampant.

We flared our wings
and were out of there.

'There's no escape,' he yelled.
'Whatever you can do I...'

and threw himself out of the window
over the balcony

and landed flat on his face.
His bones were crushed, the ground
awash with his cursed blood.

Pyreneus's hot breath is still on our necks,
he stalks our dreams.

IV. Now You See It

'Confusion now hath made his masterpiece'

After the shy ones,
there were pushy daffodils,
flagrant tulips. Overnight,

spring leapt from the conjuror's cabinet
like the lovely woman
in a kerfuffle of leafage and blossom,

an *enfant terrible*
spring-heeled as a lamb
and clamorous with initiatives,

making a helluva racket
with its randy birds and lawnmowers
and rampant gardens that are bloody hard work.

It's a season of prolepses and throw-backs,
the dithery interim between stasis and torpor,
an antsy time

when the young man's fancy lightly turns,
as the euphemism has it, …
and we're playing strip poker with nature

and peel off our layers
as cherry and almond and hawthorn
shimmy their pink and white frillies.

Don't fall for these flounces and furbelows;
see them as dabs of shaving foam
fuzzing a minimalist elegance.

Our rusty machinery heaves into life
and we're off again,
plodding through all the tomorrows

in tranquil, seductive light,
in the kindest of seasons,
the saddest of seasons

for man has created death
and each leaf is flecked
with the knowledge of autumn.

Familiars

Had he ever frolicked in a scamble of kittens
or sprung, light and elastic,
from piano to bookcase,
avoiding, by a whisker, the ornaments?

Not Carlo,
an Elder Statesman from the first,
who sat all day on a window ledge,
a gourmet in a white bib
and as wise as the Owl of Cwm Cawlwyd,

an admirable creature like all of his kind,
divinely indifferent to us and our feelings,
for they are patricians

hunters, duellists, promiscuous,
who make a scrupulous toilette
before a night on the tiles
and return, dishevelled, at dawn.

Sponges of love,
yielding and frigid,
they commandeer anyone's lap
for a sensuous stroking
and their warmth is specious.

In and out they move
between hearth and nightmare,
jungle and indolence,
pounce and stealth,
thrum and screech.

We too are on edge,
feeling the soft pads,
sensing the sheathed claws.

Butterfly Brain

'What should such fellows as I do,
crawling between heaven and earth?'
(*Hamlet*)

I stood in insect-sizzling grass
beneath gambolling papery scraps
bright as Chinese lanterns,

blurred, ferocious wings,
lifetimes beaten out in a day.
Sic transit and other such thoughts.

And yet, if butterflies could take a view,
they'd pity those earth-bound creatures,

their lack of feelers for the world,
the bluntness even of the fingertips;

and how they see blue, yellow, scarlet clash
and not the thousand lovely shades of dusk;

how they're blind to the nectaries' glowing trail
beyond the violet and cannot hover

in the heady cups of flowers or suck
filigree juices from a wounded tree.

They do not quiver as, a flute from miles away,
their mate's compulsive scent
pierces the pandemonium of stinks.

Having been here so long, they can't
let it go. How poignant
their endless, insensate galumphing.

Beau Monde

They've left their bits-and-bobs in their dressing-rooms,
now take their ease in the salon, promenading
under a powder-blue ceiling, on a deep-pile green carpet:

long-headed aristocrats in conker-coloured coats
who flick their dressing-gown tassels
with a Noël Coward nonchalance.

There's all sorts: disdainful, sociable, shy
in tête-a-têtes and spats and frisky games.

Gourmets pick and choose and turn their noses up
while a chubby duchess chomps incessantly.

An addict, head plunged deep, snuffles a line.
A young one shelters by mamma: she's not yet 'out'.
A housemaid's swaddled in an old blue cloth.

What a show they put on! I admire
their frank, eighteenth-century pissing and dumping

and take away two things: the soft rise and fall
of a girl's rump on rounded flesh

and how in standing individual, gathered, still,
the horses know each other to the bone and heart.

Let His Bones Live

Reading Abbey Relics List

Capillus sancte Marie ut putantur

Glance at this list and you'd think
how charming the credulous faith
of the twelfth-century monk
who listed the splinters of wood from the Cross,
the bones and flesh of the martyrs,
fragments of cloth that wiped the Lord's sweat.

Yet as I read, in this bare room,
within yards of the place it was written,
and wonder if his task were privilege or penance,
celebration or chore, a catalogue
of miraculous salvifics
or of money-spinning gewgaws,

that old monk stirs to life,
no dryasdust or blind believer
but a sceptic ('A hair of Mary ... reputedly'),
a fanciful poet ('Jesus's umbilicus
... or foreskin?'). Surely he chuckled
at a few grains of earth dug up at Calvary

but as he handled the girdle and tunic, shreds
that had touched the most intimate places
(*noli me tangere*) of the Virgin Mother,
he was surely also dumbfounded
as each day at the altar
when bread became flesh in his hands

and then that enormous collection
of rags and of body parts
sang in his ears
and the glorious company of the Apostles
the noble army of Martyrs
appeared to his eyes.

After two hundred and thirty entries
he's had enough: 'There are yet more'
sounds just like Cromwell's man: 'A multitude
of small bonys, laces, stonys and ermys
wiche wolde occupie iiij schetes of papyr
to make particularly an inventory of every part thereof'.

And down the centuries,
from that treasury of faith,
I hear him bless the Lord
and from that dust heap
I catch the whisper
of boredom, doubt, despair.

Now You See It

Ai Weiwei, *Dropping a Han Dynasty Urn*
(triptych of black-and-white prints) 1995

Would you want –
this is not a rhetorical question –

to balance between your finger-tips
a Han Dynasty Urn,
the flaring lip, the swelling body

to widen by an insignificant distance
the gap between right hand and left

to thrill with your own helplessness
at the urn's irreversible descent
past chest, thighs, knees

to stand, hands apart,
the fragments at your feet

to have done something irretrievable,
autonomous, wicked?

*

Couldn't you admire the man
who had the balls,

who did it
who presents himself, the guilty party

before the firing squad of our eyes
with his crazed abracadabra?

*

We wanted a recuperation,
to see it reassemble

piece by piece
rise through the air to the hands' nest

wanted someone to tell us
the photograph was doctored,
the urn a cheap modern fake

that we share no genes with the millions
who've shattered statues, burned books.

from *Cutting the Quick* (2005)

How I Dealt with Uncle George's Glass Eye

was to skid from teastain islands on the tablecloth
to canyons in the plaster overhead
or troll it in the gutter with my ally taw
or drop the pale blue yolk and creamy white
into a frying-pan. Our laughter
made the birthday candles genuflect.
His mouth and left eye shone.
The right was as indifferent as the stars.

The Glass

You pause
and it's stilled
in the air between us

a scatter of gleams
in a shout of sunlight

your breath on my cheek
condensed to a razor-thin tulip

sand raging like stars,
annealed to a million-year crawl

Out of Sight

When I came across your photograph,
I knew I'd not forgotten for a moment,
in three years, the crinkle of your upper lip,
and how your finger-nail had traced
a vein along my arm. The mind is not
a shoe-box storing bric-a-brac
but stained and leaded glass
whose reds and yellows flare up in the sun.

L'histoire centrale

The woman with the grey cloth over her head,
one hand behind a tuba,

has no need of the reticent suitcase
and its cargo of, let's say, louche

camisoles, canaries, cinnamon, its odour
of excitable gunpowder.

When I came across Magritte's *L'histoire centrale*,
the long, dumb wail,

there was no reason on earth it reminded me
of you

plaiting your words with mine
as we watched the skirmishing rain

from the door of the Rudolfinum concert hall
while Brahms and Mahler's swell

drained through talk of *Don Giovanni*,
Arcimboldo, Rosicrucian alchemy

to beer and the backstreets of Prague.
The street lights splotched your rouge.

You whispered that the heart was india-rubber.
The twinkly Vltava was sheeted lead.

Taking Leave

No one looked up when she typed the last letter,
aligned the things on her desk and drove
the mute streets unreeling red lights,
patterns of neon, scissor men, girls with teeth
until the car slowed itself, stopped
among shuttered families, dead lawns.
Sidesaddle on a low brick wall,
one sheer-stockinged leg crossed on the other,
the midnight blue dress buttoned to her throat,
bracelets at ankle and wrist, hair rigid and waved:
something lifted from a dressmaker's window,
a tulip, unopened, in the unending street.
Eyes bright and blank as a bird's.
The poplars, behind her, are fuzzy with spring.
Across town no-one noticed
the light that didn't come on.
It's raining sweetly, steadily inside her head.

A Cubist Notebook on Cézanne

He painted apples. There they are:
eighteen reddish orange, greenish yellow spheres,
lodged on hidden coins.
A wicker basket on a table top,
tipped on a block of wood.

*

Monet was just an eye
that caught on gleams.
Cézanne, too, painted surfaces.
Mottled russets, a blotch of green,
a primrose swipe: snug, now,
to the mind's hand, indestructible.

*

Birds aren't fooled. A harmony
of paint's no harmony of fruit.

*

It's thinkable to put a price-tag
on an apple in a cornucopia.
To stick one on an apple by Cézanne
's absurd, like asking Mona Lisa round for tea.

*

He left himself aside. No one
paints apples like Cézanne.

*

The eye keeps coming back to
what it's seeing
for the first time now.

*

He spied with his concentric eye
the world's geometry.

*

Grumpy, diabetic, getting old,
slave to his eye,
to obstinate paint.

    *

His eye was rinsed. It stripped
the mouldy skins: the bulging Horn,
the Vanitas, the plausible Tree.

    *

Each apple burns itself.
It is the sun, solidified.

    *

He swallowed all his love for them,
as Rilke said, and gave it rest in paint.

from *Nothing's Lost* (2014)

Peregrine

She floats to hand, hooks to the leather fist
like that other self he sees in the mirror,
inches from his eyeballs and a world away.

His craft and will against her flint,
her slate feathers, notched beak,
fathomless, coalpit eyes.
He works her with hoodwink and lure.

Nothing's gentler than the manning
as he smooths her head with a feather,
nothing's more delicate
than the two-tone tinkle
of bells as she glides to a treetop.

He feels, far back,
how his hand balanced a spear,
how his belly warmed
to the ribbon of blood.

Whatever it is that rises from the long grass
at two hundred yards is dead already.
Her stoop shears the sky,
pure and inhuman as Aldebaran.

Not for her the hawk's swerve
to the tossed gobbet. She'll biff
a rook like a bullet, grab and rip
like a machine, strip life
to the bone, like poetry.

He thrills to that truthfulness,
its cold, transparent tarn; longs
for her life of pounce and gorge,
of lazing and killing; worships
one untrammelled by love or pity.

Silver Bream

How sexy bream are,
industrious lap dancers
in slinky chainmail,
silverleaf bodystockings,
always, always on the move:
mouth, muscles, gills and fins.

The Blind Watchmaker,
patient as Dürer,
tiled these flanks,
dropped each granulated
blob of solder into place.

In this nanomachinery
the eye is a hulking washer,
the pupil a black hole.

There is sadness in fish,
in the tearable flesh
of the mouth and the gills.

Look long enough,
one becomes a friend,
a little old man, pursing
and puffing his thick lips.
Is his speechlessness
empty-headed or wise?
His world's laid bare
but he's as other
as angels or trilobites.

The tank's Grand Central:
each fish, driven by hunger
on its course, defers to each.

The patterns are traceless
strolls in a watery park.
If there were souls,
they'd dance like this
to a wandering flute,
octaves beyond us.

When the music stops,
nothing's more dead
than the walleyed mouth gape
of a fish dropped on a slab
or stuffed in a case.

Light and Shade

At first I took them for sculptures:
on one bank the angler
studious over his rod,
his eye on the float,
on the other an unruffled
wedding-guest, a young heron

but stood long enough
to see the man rub his thumb
on the rod's cork handle,
try a sandwich, pick up another,
scratch his nape,
glance at the seething gentles

while the heron was stone-still
but for repetitive, mechanical head-flicks.
Millions of years had pared
the dagger bill, the repertoire.
I wanted his yellow searchlight eye,
his stillness before lightning

then thought: better a brilliant, cleared sky
or clouds and their nuances?

Masterstroke

Your feet follow the dips and bends
of the towpath or the lie of the grass,
rushes are bent into huts and hairdos,
catkins flirt in the breeze,

a coot snails upstream
on a diagonal, half-drifting,
half fighting the current
so its bill misses nothing,

the wind teases a flickering
network of light from the water
to a boat's white bow:
a galaxy forming and fading.

The oarsman, headed wherever,
inscribing the watery steppe,
looks for eddies and snags,
for advantages. Water submits

to muscle and will, to the robotic pull
of the blades, the swift scissors
till on the bend, as he feathers,
stilled, poised in his shell,

he's the keystone that locks into one
clouds, willows, water-birds, river.

A Georgian Wineglass

Sand and fire,
fusion's rage,
split-second gather and blow,
swing and spin of the pipe.

A slip of a thing,
water and air,
mizzle-coloured,
breath visible.

The eye loiters
from foot to stem
to flaring trumpet,
skates the rim.

The one tear is for
its unbearable beauty,
the pontil's hidden
unavoidable scar.

One for the Birds

Straight out of Pliny, I grant you,
but true nonetheless:

I was in Room 30 of the National Gallery
last Wednesday, when a pigeon walked in

on finicky toes, flicking her button eyes
from sour Martha to slumped Christ to John

seeing things on the Island of Patmos.
She too saw what she wanted:

a cup of water. I loved
the solid, canvas-coloured cup,

the glisten of light on the rim,
the sliver of limpid water, symbolizing—

so I'd read—the Virgin's purity.
The pigeon rose like a delighted child,

chivvied the water with her beak, and departed
on derisive, whistling wings.

Looking at Morandi

When I see these pale flasks, bottles, jars
    at the edge of a table
a cityscape unchanging monumental

always now it's a Sunday one December
when a pane of glass, four foot square, wobbles,
starts – will it? – to fall
and my hand dithers
            and the pane's not 'frozen'
but simultaneously falling and receding
(a willed, hopeless re-winding)
in a moment that's no time at all
            and longer than lasting
till someone I find to be me
has his right hand clamped round the thumb of his left
which is ripped (almost off? to the bone?)
and senses already the unending sequelae
of stitches, infection, night nurses,
the weeks-long ebbing of purple and yellow
(compacted by memory to moments)

and a flask's in mid-air,
drenched in crimson.

Giorgio Morandi, 1890–1964, Italian painter

Here and Now

    I'm wishing I could be Frank O'Hara and stop for
a cheeseburger and chocolate malted at JULIET'S CORNER
and watch the girls' skirts blow up over grates and the Puerto
Ricans stand about on the avenue
    or Ginsberg deep in the watermelons and avocados and
brilliant cans of a California supermarket
    but there's nothing to do or to see because it's eleven
o'clock on a morning in mid-January in Reading, England and
the sky's grey and the rain only just holding off and the wind
gusting under the narrow sky
    and in the purple-framed windows of Moonstone's Gifts
and Crafts the salt lamps are tired and crystals hang dispiritedly
and there's a plastic Gandalf
    and opposite there's the vast dirty redbrick fortress
of Brock Barracks and a public lavatory, boarded-up, and it's
cold and I'm coughing in the wind and hurry past the Polish
Delikatesy,
    the halal meats, the Tabernacle of the God of Prophecy
(once a bank), a benign Sikh, Caribbean Supreme Cuisine
('1 piece chicken + rice'), a line of rubbish bins throwing up,
two smiling (Japanese?) girls in leggings, pink and orange
    to peer in at Afro and European Human Hair where
a woman hunts for a colour match among the plastic-sheathed
scalpings hung round the walls.
    The whole world's nested here: nose flutes, maracas,
hypnotic tablas, notes scattered on the freezing wind; almost,
when you listen, a symphony.
    High over the hard and glittery porcelain of Bathroom
Collection there's the faded elegant black lettering of Dunlop's
Hay & Straw Factors and briefly wagons creak and horses drop
steaming dung under the eyes of men with watch chains.
    In fuggy Costa Coffee an old woman tells herself she
wants a glass of hot lemon with sugar and asks an empty chair,
'Where did you go on holiday?' and blesses me with a smile.

    Outside, a spaceship has landed and thrusts its gold antenna at the sky. And next to the mosque there's a sex shop's chaste windows.
    Time now to catch the bus somewhere between the greengrocer's, where the sun lights for a moment limes, Turkish peppers, guavas so that they gleam as if with little bulbs inside
    and House Clearance next door, the sediment and history of suffering, laughter, lives: sofas and paintings, dinner plates, board games, photo frames.

Crushed Velvet

When he talked to the dresses she'd taken, his hands
  smoothed velvet, slid on silk.
He threw out the hangers, their sad shoulders. Like a photographic
  negative
absence made her real near a phantom table, the glimmer
  of a chair.
Even when he'd gone through the house, he came across
  a hairgrip,
her *Copper Fire* lipstick, a note at the back of a drawer. He dreamt
of a rubbish tip piled with her shopping bags and Simone de Beauvoir,
her copies of *Cosmo*, the ironic pink eggcup. He burnt what
  he could
and hammered the rest. One day, by the furrowing sea,
  his stick
wrote her name in the sand. He watched the tide swirl the grains
to wherever, because of the writing, they'd go. Though things smash
to smithereens and the fusions of memory, nothing's lost. They'd stood
  once
in a strange light in a flooded meadow as a white horse, leading her
  foal,
picked her way across a violet wash, hoof by high-stepping hoof.

Nightfall

At age fourteen, he said,
he'd locked the bathroom,
cleaned his teeth,

looked into the mirror
and aimed the gun

into that other mouth.
We heard the starburst glass,

his sisters banging on the door,
a voice running the stairs

and saw the blue revolving light,
the shaking boy

and did not ask him why
but sipped our coffee,

watching the reflections
as the windows darkened
and the lamps blinked on.

Gogol on the Loose

They opened his coffin and found
what remained of him, supine,
claw marks on the lid's underside,
and remembered he'd been cataleptic.
Don't think of him waking, whispering,
of his eyes opening, re-opening,
of his fingers tracing the satin cocoon,
of the screams the owls heard.
                          Think of his nose,
that magnificent hooter, so long and droopy
his lower lip reached it. Picture that ripsnorting
nose as it floats through woodwork and soars
over squadrons of angels and generals
for one last sniffing-out of Moscow,
one last, delirious strafing
of apparatchiks and jobsworths,
of bureaucrats, bullionaires, lickspittles.
Think how that irrepressible and promiscuous nose
will weep for men at the back doors of restaurants,
for the woman who buys one tomato,
for the waitress who's dusting, leaf by leaf,
a plastic birch.
                That piteous nose will drape
round the shoulders of Akaky Akakiyevich
as he squats in the lee of a monastery wall,
sucking the neck of a bottle, a new overcoat,
quilted, double-seamed, with silk-lined hood.

Electroplate

Any number of umbrellas and girlfriends,
both parents, a ceramic bowl, swirling
orange and turquoise and biscuit

like the clouds of a gas giant: all gone,
just twinges. What wakes me at four
is knowing that my memory's wired to a cathode,

that a thin, incessant rain of words
falls on my past, that I can't,
for example, remember, for the life of me,

how it felt when Masha pulled on her boots
in the foyer of the Novaya Opera
(the shape of her smile, the curve of her back)

because what's taken its place is my poem,
the moment's epitaph and tombstone:
'She smiles as, slowly, she zips them'.

The thick-fleshed roach I've landed down the years,
which thumped on the bank and whiplashed in my hands,
have turned into tinplated knick-knacks.

Notes

Moment
Alessandra Gerardi, *Glance* (photograph)

The Spotted Veil
Manet, *Young Woman in a Round Hat*

Et in Arcadia Ego
The phrase is Anon. Often found on tombs in paintings, most famously in Poussin's *The Arcadian Shepherds* in the Louvre. The poem rests on both possible meanings: that I, the tomb's occupant, was once in Arcadia and that I, Death, am in Arcadia.

Afterlife
The shoes are in the Museum of English Rural Life, Reading. I am grateful to the curators for information about them. Certain personal items, such as shoes, were often preserved, sometimes walled-up, to protect a house against evil spirits.

Going
A haibun. A prose form stemming from Basho, recording the significant moments of a journey, outer or inner, concluded by a poem in the spirit of a haiku.

What Did You Take Away?
A friend's question I answered after visiting a mill in Castle Cary, Somerset, one of only two factories in the world still weaving fabrics from horsehair.

My Idle Guitar
Wallace Stevens's visit to Florida in 1919 stayed with him for the rest of his life.'Nomad Exquisite', a self-deprecating description, is the title of a poem that records his response to the intensity and beauty of natural life in Florida. The guitar was an important instrument in his poetry (and in his life).

The Exile: Mr Stevens at the Barber's
The poem imagines Wallace Stevens visiting a barber's in London. Stevens became Vice-President of the Hartford Accident and Indemnity Company. The phrases that bewilder the barber come from Stevens's poems. The last two lines are adapted from his great poem of exile, 'A Dish of Peaches in Russia'.

'About must, and about must goe'
The poem quotes from or alludes to Donne, Herbert, Eliot and Yeats, four poets I have loved from youth to age.

Possession
The painting was in *Australia*, an exhibition at the Royal Academy in 2013. The artist, born in 1953, is a clan leader and chairman of several Aboriginal organisations.

It Must Change
Throughout his life Paul Nash's paintings and drawings examined the landscape of England. A recurring subject, many approaches, responding to the movements of the times. Exploration, not restlessness. An example to poets? The 'It Must' titles nod to the titles of the three parts of Wallace Stevens's 'Notes toward a Supreme Fiction', which is, among all else that it is, an inquiry into the nature of the poetic imagination.

On Margate Sands
'On Margate Sands. / I can connect/ Nothing with nothing.' (*The Waste Land*). Man Ray, *Dust Breeding* (1920) (photograph). Exhibited in *Journeys with The Waste Land* at Turner Contemporary, Margate (2018).

Metamorphoses
Ovid's Metamorphoses sees the whole of Nature, and of human and divine nature, as always changing, always fluid. Its principal subject matter, sex and the relationship between the sexes, is relevant in any age and sharply relevant in our own. It seems right, therefore, that this handful of treatments should be varied: (free) translations and versions

and offshoots, written from male, female and neutral points of view. In three or four of these poems we find Ovid's recurring horror at the silencing of women.

Mutes
Met. VI. 401–674 for the story of Philomel. The recipe is abbreviated from a recipe at Basildon Park, a Georgian mansion near Reading.

Javelins
Met. II.401–530.Callisto, a nymph raped by Jupiter and turned into a bear by Juno. Arcas, her unwitting son, encountered the bear on a hunting expedition.

Europa and the Bull
Met. II.833–75. The beginning and end are a free translation. The paintings by Boucher and Titian are in the Wallace Collection in London.

Peleus's Story
Met. XI.221–265. The rape of the nymph Thetis, re-told from Peleus's point of view. Thetis had inherited her shape-shifting powers from her father, Proteus. The child of the union was Achilles.

One or the Other or Neither or Both
Met. IV.285–388.Ovid's tale is about female passion and is onomastic, an explanation of why men who bathe in this pool become effeminate. The present version speaks to a contemporary issue.

Pyreneus and the Muses
Met. V.269–293.Pyreneus, the pursuer of the Muses, might well be seen as the enemy of the expressive arts

Two Rivers Press has been publishing in and about Reading since 1994. Founded by the artist Peter Hay (1951–2003), the press continues to delight readers, local and further afield, with its varied list of individually designed, thought-provoking books.